T0035954

How to
BIRD

Rasha Hamid

free spirit
PUBLISHING®

Copyright © 2024 by Rasha Hamid

All rights reserved under International and Pan-American Copyright Conventions. Unless otherwise noted, no part of this book may be reproduced, stored in a retrieval system, or transmitted in any form or by any means, electronic, mechanical, photocopying, recording or otherwise, without express written permission of the publisher, except for brief quotations or critical reviews. For more information, go to freespirit.com/permissions.

Free Spirit, Free Spirit Publishing, and associated logos are trademarks and/or registered trademarks of Teacher Created Materials. A complete listing of our logos and trademarks is available at freespirit.com

Library of Congress Cataloging-in-Publication Data
Names: Hamid, Rasha, author.
Title: How to bird / Rasha Hamid.
Description: Minneapolis, MN : Free Spirit Publishing, an imprint of Teacher Created Materials [2023] | Audience: Ages 3–8
Identifiers: LCCN 2023007257 (print) | LCCN 2023007258 (ebook) | ISBN 9798885540346 (hardback) |
ISBN 9798885540353 (ebook) | ISBN 9798885540360 (epub)
Subjects: LCSH: Bird watching—Juvenile literature. | BISAC: JUVENILE NONFICTION / Social Topics / New Experience |
    JUVENILE NONFICTION / Diversity & Multicultural
Classification: LCC QL677.5 .H26 2023 (print) | LCC QL677.5 (ebook) | DDC 598.072/34—dc23/eng/20230420
LC record available at https://lccn.loc.gov/2023007257
LC ebook record available at https://lccn.loc.gov/2023007258

Free Spirit Publishing does not have control over or assume responsibility for author or third-party websites and their content. At the time of this book's publication, all facts and figures cited within are the most current available. All telephone numbers, addresses, and website URLs are accurate and active; all publications, organizations, websites, and other resources exist as described in this book; and all have been verified as of April 2023. If you find an error or believe that a resource listed here is not as described, please contact Free Spirit Publishing. Parents, teachers, and other adults: We strongly urge you to monitor children's use of the internet.

Edited by Alison Behnke
Cover and interior design by Courtenay Fletcher
Photos by Rasha Hamid, Anna Jeffers, Katie Rust, Ruben Giron, and iStock.com

Printed by: 70548
Printed in: China
PO#: 9093

Free Spirit Publishing
An imprint of Teacher Created Materials
9850 51st Avenue North, Suite 100
Minneapolis, MN 55442
(612) 338-2068
help4kids@freespirit.com
freespirit.com

For Jibreel and every birder made
to feel unwelcome in public spaces.
We belong.
—R.H.

Are you a **birder?**

People who bird are called birders. Birders notice and observe wild birds in their habitats.

Anyone can bird.

Some birders use tools to see or hear better.

glasses

binoculars

hearing aid

Other tools help birders research and record what they notice.

phone app

writing tool

field guide

paper

camera

YOU.

When you're ready to bird, put on your birding outfit. (Check the weather first!)

Take any tools you might use.

If you can, go to places with trees or water. Many birds prefer natural spaces, but you will see birds in most outdoor places.

Plant your feet.

Take a deep breath.

Barred owls
Hoot Hoot
"who cooks for you."

Mourning doves
sing a sad
cooOOwoo wOOwOO song.

Woodpeckers
Chirp and
Cackle.

TAP! TAP!

Chickadees
sing
chickadee deedee.

House sparrows
loudly sing

Tweet Tweet Tweet!

Red-winged
blackbirds
sound like a
referee's whistle!

Listen.

Blue jays **shriek, whistle, chirp, whir** and **gurgle.**

Geese **HONK HONK,** like a clown-car traffic jam!

Cardinals **whistle** and sometimes sound like a **laser!**

Male wood ducks sound like a zipper **zipppping** really fast.

Gaze at the ground.

Scan tree trunks and branches.

Look for contrasting **colors**

and bird-shaped **silhouettes.**

Look along ledges, around rooftops, and across any kind of water.

Watch for movement.

Look up.

Different birders have different **superpowers.**

Some are great at spotting movement or color.

Other birders tune in to every sound.
Some count birds so quickly!

And some memorize
hundreds of bird songs.

The more you bird, the more you'll learn about your own birding superpowers.

You might see something
extraordinary.

When you do, celebrate quietly so you don't scare the birds!

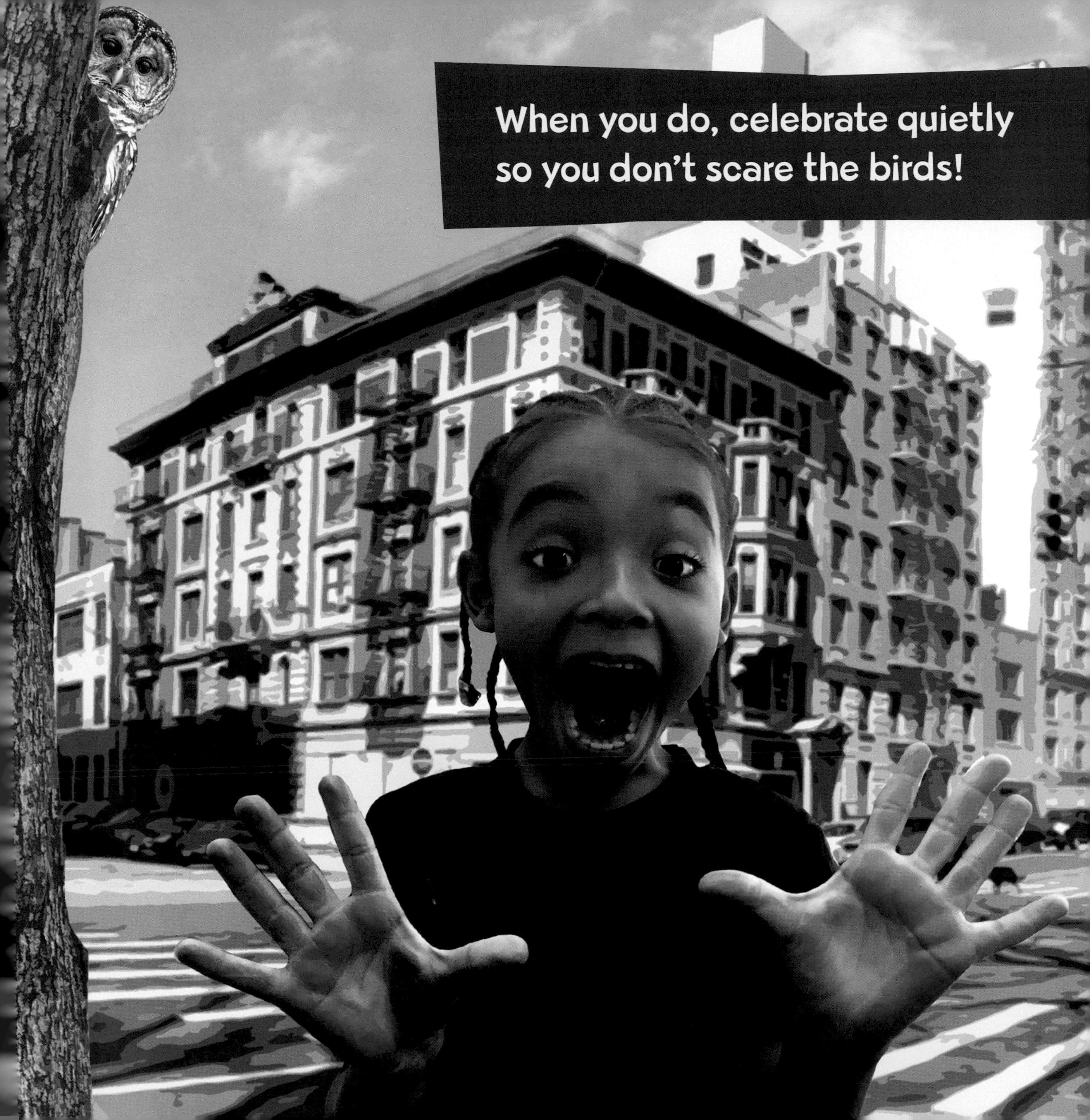

Record what you observe. You can draw a bird, write a poem, take a picture, or make a list. How will *you* remember what you noticed?

Now you know how to bird.

Happy birding!

A Note from Rasha

Dear Readers,

Birding is one of my special interests. It makes me feel peaceful and joyful. Every time I go birding in the park near my home in New York City, I see something amazing—a great blue heron fishing, a barred owl taking flight, or red-tailed hawks soaring and diving! The more I practice, the better I get at spotting birds.

Seeing and hearing many species of birds has been proven to make people happier. And spending time in nature can make people healthier. Unfortunately, in some neighborhoods there aren't enough green spaces. Areas that don't have enough parks are sometimes called *park deserts*. In places with few green spaces, there are also fewer birds.

Birders are every age, color, gender, ability, and size. Birders live in every part of the world and speak thousands of languages. Public green spaces are not always welcoming and accessible to everyone, but many individuals and groups are working to make birding more inclusive. Birding is for absolutely everyone. So get out there and bird!

Love,
Rasha

Questions to Think About

Whether you're a brand-new birder or you've been doing it a while, it's fun to talk about birding with other people! Here are some questions to get you started.

- What do you think your birding superpower could be?
- Who would you like to go birding with?
- What is your favorite birding outfit?
- What do you enjoy most about birding?
- How do you feel when you bird?

- How could you teach someone else how to bird?
- What is your favorite bird you've ever seen?
- Are there park deserts in your area? If so, how can you advocate for more public green spaces in your community?
- How can you help other birders feel welcome?
- How can other birders help you feel welcome?

Birding Words

advocate—to speak up or write to support a cause

bird—as a verb, this means to go looking for birds in cities, parks, forests, and other outdoor spaces

birders—people who bird

birding—the activity of looking for birds in outdoor spaces

field guide—an illustrated book for recognizing birds in nature

extraordinary—special, unusual, or amazing

habitats—the places where plants, animals, or other organisms normally and naturally live

observe—to carefully watch or notice

park deserts—urban areas without nearby green spaces

record—to write, draw, or make note of something

silhouettes—the dark shapes and outlines of bodies or other shapes

Birding and Nature Organizations to Check Out

Birdability (birdability.org) focuses on increasing the number of accessible birding spaces available to disabled birders.

The Cornell Lab of Ornithology (birds.cornell.edu/home) learns about, teaches about, and conserves biological diversity through research, education, and bird-focused community science.

The Feminist Bird Club (feministbirdclub.org) works to promote inclusivity in birding and helps diverse communities connect with the natural world.

New York City's Urban Park Rangers (nycgovparks.org/programs/rangers) help community members and visitors explore NYC parks through programming including environmental education, wildlife management, and conservation.

Outdoor Afro (outdoorafro.org) celebrates and inspires Black connections and leadership in nature.

Do you think you can spot all the birds in this book? Visit go.freespirit.com/bird to download a list of the birds that appear.

About the Author and Photographer

Rasha Hamid attended New York City public schools before earning a bachelor's degree in Africana Studies and Education at Vassar College and a master's degree in Special Education at Bank Street College of Education. Rasha has developed her practice in classrooms in East Harlem, Hamilton Heights, Khartoum, and Brooklyn for over twenty years. Rasha considers herself an educator-activist—someone who works to make the world more just, joyful, equitable, and sustainable through the education of students and teachers. She began creating picture books with her classes to fill the need for books reflecting her students, their experiences, and their passions. Many of the photos in this book were taken by Rasha—and many of them are of students she knows. Rasha is proud to be the autistic mom of an autistic young adult. Autism and birding are two of Rasha's special interests.